The Stateless Millionaire
Life's Lessons on How to Build Your Finances from Zero to Millions

Dr. Ali Abkar

Copyright © 2023 Dr. Ali Abkar

All rights reserved. No part of this book should be reproduced by duplicating, expanding, shortening, or paraphrasing it without the author's permission. This work is intellectual property, and any copyright violation would be treated as a violation of the law.
ISBN: 978 – 1 – 960207 – 35 – 7

DISCLAIMER

As you brace yourself for an exciting ride be warned, preserving certain information and the author's security means that some places and countries have been named differently. In addition, the order of events has been altered.

As you read on, you will discover you can learn valuable lessons from dictators. Hitler himself once said, "Truth is a lie repeated often!"

Before you turn the final page, let me dedicate this book to the courageous women of Iran. These women continue to fight for their rights, freedom, and lives. This is for Women, for Life, for Freedom!

DEDICATION

Listen up, all you ambitious dreamers and go-getters!

This book is for YOU. It's time to kick-start your journey toward financial success, no matter where you're starting from. Let it ignite the fire within you and give you the tools to achieve your wildest dreams.

These pages provide guidance, motivation, and practical advice to realize your financial aspirations. It's time to take action, never give up, and build the life you truly desire.

Are you ready to become a stateless millionaire? Let this book be your guide on this exhilarating journey.

Table of Contents

Getting Your Feet Wet: Tough Time Make Tough People 8
A Million Miles from the Middle East 8
Failing Health 8
From Zero to Million People 8
Adding it Up 8
What's the Concept of a Stateless Millionaire and Where Does it Begin? 8
You Won't Make Money Until You Make Up Your Mind to Make Money 8
The Dream of Every Immigrant 8
Money Does Not Make a Man. The Mind Does. 8
The Success so Far 8
Before You Flip Over. Here's a Snappy Task Specifically for You 8
The Passion Paycheck: Why Pursuing What You Love Is the Greatest Place to Start 8
Cut out for Something Great 8
Is the World About to Wake Up to the Need for Passion? 8
Let's clear it up 8
The Stateless Millionaire Follows His Passion 8
Straight Talk: Striking a Balance Between Passion and Paycheck 8
Let's Do this 8
Separating what matters from what does not is the key to everlasting wealth. 8
The Lesson Learned 8
The American Debt Culture 8
How Real can it Get? What are Credit Statistics Saying? 8

The Stateless Millionaire Understands Debt, All the Way Through 8
Why Do You Want to Make Millions? 8
What're Your Motives? 8
The Stateless Millionaire knows Why 8
A Perspective on Money You Won't Find in Other Personal Finance Books 8
The Stateless Millionaire Knows He's the Greatest Capital 8
Financial Discipline: Lessons Learned from Stock Market Investing. 8
The All-too-Important Question 8
The Principle that Works for All 8
Why does it matter? 8
Money Moves towards People in Motion 8
It was Time to Act 8
The Stateless Millionaire Makes Money Moves 8
The Stateless Millionaire Gives Back 8
It's Can't Get Simpler 8
Is it Wrong to Keep Money Aside for Sunny Days 8
I Know Better 8
The Eight Myths About Saving 8
Savings prioritize your future over short-term expenses. 8
The Stateless Millionaire Saves and Use it Wisely 8
Stateless Millionaires Leverage Financial System 8
What Banks and Big Companies Like Apple Don't Want you to know About Loans 8
Mortgage and Commercial Loan 8
The bottom line 8
Adapting to Changes 8
The Stateless Millionaire is Adaptative 8

The Stateless Millionaire Creates Value at Every Turn 8
What is Value Creation 8
Stateless millionaires choose excellence. 8
Do you think you can do much without being excellent? 8
Excellence Means Soft Skills Also. 8
The power of Focus 8
Taking the Shot Thereafter 8
You Can't Do Everything. 8
Have a Target in Your Work and Business. It Saves the Stress of Pursuing What's Not 8
Multi-tasking 8
The Stateless Millionaire is Focused 8
Diversification 8
Fear or Gain: Which Comes First? 8
Helpful Tips on Diversifying I learned 8
The Stateless Millionaire is Diverse 8
Finding the Land of Opportunity 8
Moving to Dubai 8
What Am I Saying in Essence? 8
The Stateless Millionaire is an Opportunist 8
Finally, on this 8
Conclusion 8
ABOUT THE AUTHOR 8
I'm Dr. Ali Abkar: Allow Me to Tell you How to Use this Book 1

ACKNOWLEDGMENTS

To all the extraordinary individuals who helped to bring this book to life, I want to shout from the rooftops: thank you, thank you, thank you!

Firstly, I owe an immense debt of gratitude to my family. They have been my biggest cheerleaders throughout this journey. You guys stuck with me in my darkest hours.

I can't forget my fantastic friends and colleagues who provided invaluable insights and feedback. Your contributions helped shape my ideas and refine my message. You're the true MVPs (Most Valuable Players)!

My editor deserves a special mention for his expert guidance, thoughtful suggestions, and incredible attention to detail. Your tireless work has undoubtedly made this book the highest quality it can be.

Last but not least, I want to thank all the readers who have taken the time to dive into these pages and learn from my experiences. I hope the lessons I have shared will empower you to build your finances from zero to millions and help you achieve your wildest dreams.

Thank you all for your tireless support, and I can't wait for you to enjoy "The Stateless Millionaire."

I'm Dr. Ali Abkar: Allow Me to Tell you How to Use this Book

Hey peeps. My name is Ali Abkar, and I'm human - just like you. But I'm not your average Joe. This book is not your average finance book. You won't find generic advice about investing in Apple or climbing the corporate ladder to become CEO. Nope, that's not my style.

I'm a neurologist, a former business owner, and a stock market failure. I've stumbled and fallen in public, ruined my clothes, fought with the dictatorial government, and battled sickness. I've made millions. And now, I'm here to share my secrets with you.

As you dive into this book, you'll meet me intimately. I'm not holding back - I'll tell you everything that went into making me a millionaire, the good, the bad, and the ugly. So buckle up and come with me. If you're ready to make your wealth dreams a reality, approach this book like you're boarding a train to the land of your dreams.

Getting Started

Richard Branson's humorous take on making money always appeals to me. His famous quip, "If you want to become a millionaire, start with a billion dollars and launch a new airline," is a witty reminder of the long-standing belief that it takes money to make money. The question is, to what extent is this true? On a scale of 1 to 10, I would say 99. But guess what? There is light at the end of the tunnel, and it's ten times brighter than the sun!

Looking beyond, you don't have to strain your eyes before you see the success stories of people who made thousands of dollars through real estate or by investing in weird technologies written on the hall of fame billboards. I am particularly drawn to Robert Allen's quote about being able to buy a piece of property within 72 hours anywhere in America with no money. Who would have thought this was possible? And seriously, it affirms the power of creative thinking and resourcefulness.

You might ask, "Can I become a millionaire without money?" The answer is largely up to you. How deep are your roots?

In arid regions, plants and animals evolve to develop a system adapted to survive with less water due to the challenging environment. They grow more extensive root systems.

Most authors would shy away from connecting with reality. They would rather stay in a fantasy world, missing one profound truth: the environment is arid. Without enough resources, you will be crushed by the competition. We are not in a waterfall. And only the fittest survive. Someone could inherit millions only for them to become broke a few years later. Money does not make you a millionaire. Your mindset does. The Stateless Millionaire understands the harshness of the terrain and tends to develop resilience and perseverance.

Achieving success as a stateless millionaire was anything but easy for me. I didn't guess my way to becoming it. The country I come from is unsupportive, making the journey extremely difficult. Instead of turning back, I used those challenges as motivation to be even stronger and more determined. I evolved to become resilient and creative. I know from experience that making a million dollars is not as straightforward as it sounds, even in a society like the United States.

Imagine how stunned I get when people say they struggle to make ends meet. They are buried in debt and unable to live the life they want. It's as though I'm seeing a shark in the Atlantic Ocean complaining about drought. "Come on. There's water all around you. Can't you see it, buddy?" They will wear sorry looks on their faces and be like, "You don't understand, Dr. Ali. I've got a mountain of problems, each twice as high as Everest."

Do you know what I think after several years of hearing all those crappy excuses? I think the real problem lies in their minds. They believe they can't make as much money as they desire. They have come to accept that making money is tied to location and opportunities. They think they could live better if they had better jobs and were paid more.

What if people viewed money as a game they could win – a game of chess or boxing? What if people were told they could win a lot? Will they believe? Creating the belief that you can increase your income is the key to unlocking your earning potential. You don't have to limit yourself to thinking you've got a lot of bills to settle or the traditional ways of making money. The real challenge is to turn that belief into certainty and take charge of your financial situation.

In the following pages, I will coach you on how to increase your income beyond the limitations of a state. I will make you a Stateless Millionaire.

Hey, just before we head out. This is not a get-rich-quick scheme, so be ready to put in the effort and take action.

Part I

THE BASICS

Show me Your Mind

Not your Worn-out Shoes

and I

Will Tell You How far

You Will Go.

1

Getting Your Feet Wet: Tough Time Make Tough People

"The gem cannot be polished without friction, nor man perfected without trials." – Confucius.

Challenges are like weights at the gym; they may feel heavy and uncomfortable at first, but they have the power to build our strength and shape our muscles. The same is true in life; challenges are not meant to break but to transform us.

Think about it: would you be the person you are today if you hadn't faced any difficulties in life? Maybe not. Challenges help us grow and evolve into the most valuable version of ourselves.

Here's a glimpse of my story.

A Million Miles from the Middle East

Growing up in Iran, my reality was far from the glamorous images of Persian carpets and ancient ruins. My country is associated with terrorism, discrimination against women, social unrest, injustice, and political instability. I have witnessed the placards, protests, and human rights violations that make headlines. I lived in a constant state of detest. The unrest in my country elicited a dread that permeated every aspect of my life. I could never tell what would happen to me. The dictatorial republic of Iran governed my every move. I longed for financial independence, free from government control.

It seemed like a far-off dream. I achieved it - I became a stateless millionaire. The dread that permeated every aspect of my life was replaced with peace and freedom. No longer was my every move governed by the dictatorial Islamic Republic of Iran.

I can now live the life I want, regardless of economic or geopolitical conditions. And the most fun part? I can pursue my goals with confidence and purpose, knowing I have financial security.

I want to clarify that my journey toward becoming a stateless millionaire wasn't driven by ill feelings toward my country or its religion. I'm a devout Muslim, and I respect all religions.

My decision to pursue financial independence was driven by a desire to live free from constant detestation and unrest in my country. I wanted to be able to pursue my goals and live my life without being governed by a dictatorial and suffocating regime.

Financial independence is a universal goal, regardless of background, religion, or nationality. It's about the freedom to pursue your passions and live a life you admire.

At this point, I think I should set the record straight. As a person exposed to diverse cultures and beliefs, I believe in treating everyone with respect and kindness, irrespective of their background. Unfortunately, Islam has been unfairly subjected to misconceptions and stereotypes that lead to unjust discrimination. That's why I want to be clear: I don't have anything against Islam.

It's frustrating to see how people judge others based on their religious beliefs without trying to understand or learn about them. We need to work harder to educate ourselves and dispel these stereotypes.

But seriously, my options were severely limited. I was constantly reminded of my place in society and the expectations that came with it. I couldn't express my thoughts and feelings openly, as doing so could lead to severe consequences. And in the eyes of the world, I was just a rebel, a troublemaker.

The Iranian government controls every aspect of your life. Limited internet access and complicated visa applications leave you feeling trapped and confined, with no way out.

The restrictions don't end here. Without worrying about government codes and regulations, you can't even have a business idea. It's as if the government is always at your neck.

As soon as you step outside Iran, you realize that the challenges don't stop at the border. Everywhere you turn, you are trailed by harmful misconceptions about Iranians that seem impossible to shake off. No matter where you turn, people label you as an Islamic extremist, a sexist who oppresses women, or even worse, a terrorist. These unfair stereotypes are like a weight you carry wherever you turn.

To be sure, an Iranian traveling outside the country faces a landslide of challenges. It's not just about packing your bags and hopping on a plane. I've had to face unfriendly visa limitations, financial sanctions, and cultural differences that can feel like an uphill battle. Political tensions and security concerns between Iran and other countries often result in visa restrictions and travel bans for Iranians, which can be frustrating. Differences in customs, language, and social norms make it challenging to adapt to new environments and connect with others. Being in a foreign place where you don't quite fit in can be depressing.

I had a tough time accessing financial amenities due to monetary sanctions. Conducting business or transferring funds abroad was a living hell. I would not get a Mastercard or a loan without answering a million questions. It felt like the whole world was against me.

It was in the midst of all this that I arose, weaving my way from the bare bottom to the top. Having sustained bruises and indelible scars, I received the most devastating news.

Failing Health

I received the dreaded news that no one ever wants to hear. I was diagnosed with cancer. It was a life-altering moment that made me confront my mortality and put everything else on hold.

As I absorbed the news, my mind raced with questions about my future. I was filled with dread. I was forced to ask myself if I hadn't suffered enough: I had been bedridden as a child because of a poor immune system. Staying in bed, unable to go around like the other kids, hurt. With an unbroken spirit, I overcame these challenges. And in adulthood, when I thought I would breathe the fresh air of relief, I got the news that blew up in a million pieces.

It was a struggle to swallow. But I knew I had to remain strong and fight this disease with all my strength.

The journey toward recovery was exhausting, and the treatments were painful, but I was determined to persevere. There were days when I felt I could not carry on a moment longer and I wanted to give up. But the support of my loved ones kept me on track. They stood by me.

Each day, I gained more strength and began to see a glimmer of hope. The treatments were working, and I was gradually getting better. Despite the obstacles I faced, I refused to let cancer define me. I was still pursuing my dreams, achieving financial success, and living the life I wanted to live.

Today, I am proud to say that I am a cancer survivor and have retraced my steps back to the top. The illness stripped me bare. I returned to be a Stateless Millionaire. The beautiful thing is that there are millions of people like me. I'd love you to meet a few of them

2

From Zero to Million People

I am about to share some inspiring stories of people who fall into the zero to million people category.

Hold onto your seats; the first person on the list is Oprah Winfrey.

Oprah Winfrey had a difficult childhood. Born into poverty in Mississippi in 1954, Winfrey was raised by her grandmother, with whom she had a challenging relationship.

But the challenges didn't stop there. Sadly, Winfrey also experienced sexual abuse during her childhood, leaving her feeling incredibly vulnerable. Winfrey shone through, and she excelled academically, earning herself a full scholarship to Tennessee State University.

From there, Winfrey launched her media career as a news anchor, and her undeniable talent and charisma eventually landed her a talk show of hers. It quickly became a massive hit, cementing her status as one of the most influential women in the world.

But Winfrey's success hasn't been all about personal gain. She has dedicated herself to supporting numerous charitable causes and advocating for social justice. Talk about using your platform for good, and you can bet Winfrey is up to it.

Hold onto your wands, the next person on the list is right here.

J.K. Rowling's journey to becoming one of the world's most beloved authors is magical.

As a single mother living in Scotland, Rowling faced more than her fair share of adversity. She was living on welfare benefits, battling depression, and had recently divorced, making it challenging to pursue her passion for writing.

Rowling refused to give up on her dreams. Even after several publishers rejected her first Harry Potter novel, she kept writing and refining her work until she finally found a publisher who saw the magic in her work.

And boy, did the world fall in love with the world of Harry Potter? The series became an instant hit, and Rowling's talent and imagination were lauded by millions of fans worldwide. Talk about a real-life hero.

Dwayne Johnson, or as we all know him, "The Rock," has one of the most inspiring stories in Hollywood. His journey to stardom wasn't a walk in the park. His family faced financial struggles and had to move frequently during childhood. To make matters worse, Johnson also endured discrimination and bullying, which would have crushed anyone's spirit.

Johnson didn't bend. He channeled his energy into sports and became a college football player. After a short stint in professional football, he turned to wrestling and quickly rose to the industry's top as one of its biggest stars.

Eventually, Johnson set his sights on Hollywood, where he carved out a successful career as an actor. He starred in numerous hit films and TV shows, making a name for himself as one of the highest-paid actors in the industry.

Adding it Up

If you thought my story was uninspiring, what about these guys' stories? They went from rock bottom to millionaire status.

There's no better time to start building your fortune and making a change.

What's the Concept of a Stateless Millionaire and Where Does it Begin?

Imagine a world where success is not defined by where you come from and where circumstances do not crush one's dreams. This is the world of stateless millionaires. They overcome poverty, discrimination, and personal tragedies to attain financial success and power. The concept of the stateless millionaire is this simple.

If you dream of becoming a stateless millionaire, then I'd be glad to tell you it begins with a step – not two steps. And you're willing to start right where you are.

Being an employee doesn't automatically disqualify you from success. One of the keys is to be mindful of every penny entering and leaving your pocket. And here's another secret - pay yourself first! This strategy can help you maintain and grow your wealth over time. But that's not all. Here are the main points to keep in mind:

- Earning an enormous salary isn't the only path to wealth.

- Being an employee doesn't hold you back either.

- Monitoring every cash flow is the most real deal you'll ever get in wealth creation.

- Paying yourself first is a sure way of growing wealth.

- Becoming a Stateless Millionaire is possible, regardless of where you are from.

3

You Won't Make Money Until You Make Up Your Mind to Make Money

My heart would race as I entered my mathematics class every day. The mere thought of my math teacher made my palms sweat and my stomach churn. His cold, intimidating demeanor and tendency to slug about the failures of the education system and the ills of the western world made me feel like I was in the middle of a Star Trek episode rather than a classroom. He wielded a sense of dictatorship over the class, and his presence instilled fear in us all.

His approach to teaching forced me to develop a poor mindset about my abilities in mathematics. I would avoid seeking help or asking questions in class, fearing ridicule and embarrassment. My grades swooped, and my confidence as a student plummeted even further.

Then one day, a new teacher arrived and took over the mathematics class. He was a small man with a big heart. He exuded warmth and friendliness, and his approach to teaching was completely different. He made math fun and engaging. He encouraged us to ask questions and seek help.

I had been conditioned to believe that math was hard and that I was not good at it. But as I began to understand the concepts and solve problems, I felt a sense of pride and accomplishment. The new teacher helped me shift my mindset from a fixed one to a growth one.

The Dream of Every Immigrant

The allure of America as the land of opportunity has been a driving force for generations of people seeking to better their lives. It's a place where dreams come true. For many immigrants, the United States represents a chance to start anew, leaving behind the hardships of their home countries and forging a new path.

I had always dreamed of coming to America, and now that I was finally here, I was filled with excitement and anticipation. Over time, I realized my dreams of living in America were inaccurate.

Life in America is often far more complex and challenging than many newcomers anticipate. The excitement of moving to a new country can quickly fade into disillusionment and frustration as the realities of day-to-day life dawn on you. The high cost of living, the competitive job market, and the difficulties of navigating a new culture can all take their toll.

This is true for immigrants from countries with vastly different socioeconomic systems and cultural norms. For many, they think there are diamonds in the alleys. In their view, America is a place where money flows freely.

Being a first-generation Iranian immigrant, I understand firsthand the challenges of starting a new life in the United States. Like many others, I was filled with hope and excitement when I first arrived, but I soon realized that my path to success would not be easy.

I struggled to find a job, make friends, and adjust to the culture. I started to feel discouraged and overwhelmed, and I began to doubt whether I had made the right decision in coming to America.

I started with menial jobs to make ends meet. At this time, I had an education and qualification back home, but my lack of fluency in English and my unfamiliarity with the job market made it difficult to find work that suited my skill set.

I started doing odd jobs, washing dishes in a restaurant and cleaning houses for wealthy families. The work was tiring, and I often felt undervalued, but I knew it was necessary to support myself and my family.

I remember feeling trapped and hopeless, struggling to survive on the meager wages I earned from my low-paying job. I was an immigrant, new to this country, and I thought this was just how life was for people like me. I saw money as a scarce resource that I had to work tirelessly to earn, and even then, it never seemed enough.

But then, one day, I met a man who would change my life forever. He was a successful entrepreneur who had immigrated to the same country as I did, and he shared his incredible story of how he had started with nothing and built a thriving business from scratch. He talked about the importance of mindset in success and how our beliefs about ourselves and our abilities can either limit or empower us.As he spoke, I felt a glimmer of hope in my heart. Maybe, just maybe, there was a way out of my current situation. Possibly, I could create a better life if I changed my mindset and believed in myself.

From that moment on, I shifted my perspective on money and success. I started to see them as abundant resources that I could attract into my life if I had the right mindset. I read books on personal development and attended entrepreneurship seminars, soaking up knowledge and inspiration.

Slowly but surely, my mindset shifted from scarcity to abundance. I started to see opportunities where I once saw obstacles, and I acted toward my goals. I started a side business and worked hard to grow it. Eventually, it became my source of income.

Today, I am grateful for mindset power. It has taught me that anything is possible if we believe in ourselves and are willing to work.

Money Does Not Make a Man. The Mind Does.

Lottery winners who squander their winnings within a few years are examples of individuals with the wrong money mindset. Many of these winners lack solid financial education and money management skills. Consequently, they tend to overspend, make poor investments, or become victims of scams and fraud. They also view money as a windfall or stroke of luck rather than a tool for building long-term wealth.

In contrast, successful entrepreneurs who have built their businesses from scratch exemplify individuals with the right money mindset. These individuals have a clear vision of their goals, a willingness to take calculated risks, and a strong work ethic.

A right-money mindset involves having a positive and proactive attitude toward finances, controlling your money, and building a healthy relationship with it. It is rooted in the understanding that money is a tool for achieving personal goals and creating a fulfilling life rather than solely accumulating wealth.

Individuals with the right money mindset embrace money as a natural part of life and recognize the importance of being knowledgeable about it. They are willing to take risks and invest in themselves, their education, and their businesses.

Another aspect of the right money mindset is developing good financial habits such as budgeting, debt management, and living below one's means. Education about personal finance and investing is not a waste. They enable you to make informed decisions about money matters.

A positive attitude toward money is like striking a goldmine. It involves overcoming guilt or shame associated with earning money and refraining from equating wealth with greed or selfishness. Instead, it means seeing money as a means to contribute to causes that matter and impact the world positively.

The Success so Far

As I continued to cultivate this mindset, I witnessed its positive impact. I could save up enough funds to purchase a business. I am now pursuing other financial objectives with renewed determination and confidence. My decision-making skills regarding finances have improved, and I feel more self-assured and empowered.

I surround myself with positive messages and role models to develop a positive money mindset. I read books on personal finance and listen to podcasts that promote financial literacy. I am connected with like-minded individuals working towards building a healthy relationship with money.

Finally, I am mindful of the language I used around money. I don't do negative self-talk and limiting beliefs and used positive affirmations and visualization to manifest my financial goals. I believe I could create wealth and economic security for myself.

Changing my beliefs about money has been a transformative experience. It has helped me to develop a positive money mindset, which has allowed me to achieve financial success.

Before You Flip Over. Here's a Snappy Task Specifically for You.

- List your present beliefs about money, including negative and positive ideas.

Reflect on how these beliefs may impact your financial situation.

- Identify any negative spending patterns by examining current expenses. Plan to address these habits and replace them with more intentional spending choices.

- Educate yourself on personal finance topics such as investing, retirement planning, and debt management to make informed decisions about your money and feel more confident in your financial choices.

- Surround yourself with people that positive influences and a healthy money mindset who can offer support and encouragement as you develop your mindset.

4

The Passion Paycheck: Why Pursuing What You Love Is the Greatest Place to Start

As I walked down the dimly lit alley, my attention was caught by a figure sitting in the shadows. As I approached, I noticed the glimmer of a silver ney (flute) in his hand. It was an odd sight - a disabled man in a wheelchair playing the flute with such grace and ease.

Despite his physical limitations, he created something beautiful. The notes filled the air and transported me to a different world as he played. It was as if the music had a life of its own, and I was lucky enough to witness it.

Months later, I was walking down a busy street when I spotted the same artist selling fruit. My heart sank. When I looked more closely, I saw the silver flute, but it was just lying down, put to no use.

Cut out for Something Great

Meeting people and sharing with them keeps me connected and alive. Even as a child, I had a natural flair for getting others interested in what I was up to. It was easy for me to gather my friends and convince them to buy a book I found in the library. But in those early stages, I didn't experience much success because even if they wanted to buy the book, they didn't have the means to.

Although my natural tendency was toward marketing, I didn't know how to pursue it full-time. I had bills to pay and no one to support me. I had to put my passion aside and look for ways to make money at the end of each month.

Is the World About to Wake Up to the Need for Passion?

It turns out that the world may finally recognize passion's value. Recent statistics show that a whopping 61% of small business owners in the US state that their primary motivation for starting their own business was to follow their passion. And the trend towards a more flexible workweek means individuals can now pursue their passions while maintaining financial stability.

Let's clear it up

Would you accept a job offer to pack snow within a square meter area for a million dollars, knowing the task could be completed in less than a day? Many individuals would not hesitate to take the job despite their personal preferences, as it offers a high salary. Yet some people wouldn't take it up before br=es.

Passion is a compelling emotion that propels individuals towards specific interests or activities. It evokes deep enthusiasm and zeal and inspires individuals to pursue their goals. Passion is typically linked to pleasure in one's pursuits. This is revealed through the desire to innovate, excel in a specific field, or explore novel experiences and challenges.

Although passion is a positive force, it may have negative repercussions if not balanced with rationality and responsibility. For instance, being preoccupied with a particular goal or activity may result in neglecting other essential aspects of one's life, such as relationships or health.

The Stateless Millionaire Follows His Passion

Have you ever been trapped in a job that pays well but leaves you empty? Many people believe that money is the ultimate motivator. However, the truth is that it's not always enough to bring happiness and fulfillment to one's career.

The Stateless Millionaires are passionate about their work and driven by a different fuel. They have an unrelenting desire to excel in their field, create something meaningful, and positively impact others. Their passion becomes their top priority, and they are willing to work extra to achieve their goals.

What sets these individuals apart is their unwavering commitment to their work. They don't just show up for a paycheck but pour their hearts and souls into every project, task, and moment of their day.

But is following your passions worth it beyond personal fulfillment? The answer is yes! When individuals follow what they love, they excel at it, leading to higher quality work and more opportunities. Passion fuels creativity, innovative ideas, and solutions, which are valuable in many industries.

The benefits don't stop there. Pursuing your passions often doesn't feel like work, making you more motivated and engaged, which leads to higher productivity and job satisfaction. This can translate into better performance and promotions, ultimately leading to financial gain.

Of course, pursuing your passions doesn't always guarantee financial success, but the rewards can be significant for those willing to put in the effort. The recent move towards a more flexible workweek acknowledges the importance of pursuing personal interests and passions. It also highlights the potential for financial gain when individuals can do what they love.

So, are you ready to join the passionate pursuit and potentially reap the financial rewards that come with it? With the world awakening to passion, now may be the perfect time to take the leap and follow your dreams.

Straight Talk: Striking a Balance Between Passion and Paycheck

Let's face it: most people don't love their jobs. More than half of employed individuals are dissatisfied with their work situation. It's a sobering fact that raises questions about the role of passion and financial stability. How can we balance the two? How can we find fulfillment in our work while paying the bills? These are essential questions that require honest answers.

It may take some time for you to find your dream job. You'll need to build connections, gain experience, and explore various options before finding the right fit. But, in the meantime, have a reliable source of income to cover your expenses. Sometimes, that might mean taking a job that's not your passion but still provides financial stability.

Set goals and develop a plan for a balance between passion and a paycheck. You need to know where you want to be in the future and create a roadmap that outlines the skills you need to acquire, the experiences you need to gain, and the people you need to meet to achieve your goals. A clear plan will help you stay motivated and focused, even when faced with obstacles.

Lastly, maintain a positive mindset and stay committed to your passions. Remember, finding a balance between force and paycheck is achievable, and it's up to you to make it happen.

Let's Do this

1. Identify your passion: Take some time to reflect on what drives you and makes you happy. Consider what you love doing in your free time and what activities bring you joy.

2. Research opportunities: Look at what kinds of careers, jobs, or industries align with your passions. Research

companies or organizations that prioritize your interests and values.

3. Develop skills: Consider taking courses or attending workshops to develop skills that align with your passion. You may also want to look at volunteering opportunities or internships to gain experience.

4. Review your goals: adapt your plans to the latest information by reviewing the financial strategies you set earlier.

5. Network: Attend networking events, connect with professionals in your desired field, and seek out mentors who can guide and support you.

5

Separating what matters from what does not is the key to everlasting wealth.

I eagerly scanned the bustling marketplace for the Ghotab, a delicious pastry that resembles the Almond Crescent snack in the United States. Finally, I spotted it and approached the vendor, requesting twelve. The vendor's eyes widened in surprise as he stared at me, wondering how I had the money to afford such a treat. But what did he know? I had just eaten three minutes earlier and craved more.

As he handed me the freshly wrapped Ghotab, I quickly hurried to a closet, desperate to savor every delicious bite without sharing it with anyone. I knew I had to be careful, as I had used the money given to me by my parents and didn't want them to find out.

Days later, I stood nervously in the hallway, waiting to board a yellow bus for a once-in-a-lifetime excursion to an art gallery in the state capital. I couldn't bring myself to tell my parents what I had done with the precious Iranian rials they had given me, and I hoped they wouldn't find out.

As I boarded the bus with my classmates, the tempting memory of the Ghotab lingered on my taste buds, reminding me of the momentary bliss I had experienced and how I got the money to buy the latest 12 wraps of Ghotab. Even though it was a small indulgence, it had brought me immense joy and satisfaction, and I knew that whenever I needed them, I would go back to my Aunty and ask her to lend me a few rials. By now, I had lost count of how much I owed her.

The Lesson Learned

Throughout our lives, we learn bit by bit, and one of the most meaningful lessons is that life is not as complicated as we make it look. Many people never learn this lesson, and I used to be one of them. I dreamt of having yachts, towering buildings, and all the material wealth one could ever imagine. I thought that was the key to happiness.

When I entered the business world, I thought it was the perfect time to enjoy the good life. I bought my first Honda SUV with cash and thought I had everything under control. But two weeks later, I had some issues with my insurance company. I had very little cash flow then, so I resorted to credit cards to bail myself out. My bills were settled, and in my head, I didn't think it was a big deal. I even asked the credit card company what limit I could go to.

I secured a loan from a credit company and eagerly embraced the American dream. My spending quickly spiraled out of control, and before long, I was buried under $50,000 in debt. Despite this, I convinced myself that I was living the life I had always wanted and continued to indulge in luxurious purchases and extravagant vacations. As the bills piled up, I realized the consequences of my actions and struggled to keep up with the payments.

I was shocked at how easily I had fallen into the trap of living with debt, convincing myself I had plenty of time to pay it off. While I was proud of my spending habits, I now saw they would not have a lasting impact. If I were to pass away that day, I would not have left anything behind that my children could cherish or benefit from. The luxurious clothes and experiences I had accumulated would likely go out of style long before they could inherit them.

The American Debt Culture

It's no longer news that Americans accumulate debt. They're living beyond their means and relying heavily on credit to fund their lifestyles. But what's causing this?

One of the primary drivers of this debt culture is easy to access to credit. With credit cards easily obtainable, individuals can accumulate debt without blinking an eye. Loans for homes, cars, and education are at one's beckon, making it easy for individuals to finance their dreams, even if they can't afford them.

Consumerism is another monster fueling debt culture. Advertisements bombard consumers with messages to buy the latest and most impressive products, promising a better life. This creates a culture where individuals feel pressured to keep up with their peers by owning the newest and most exciting things. Who wants to be left out of the party? Nobody.

American debt culture is dominated by the pressure to keep up with the Joneses. Many people want the same material possessions as their friends and neighbors to fit in and be accepted. This leads to individuals purchasing things they cannot afford and taking on debt to maintain their lifestyle.

American debt culture has negative consequences for individuals and society. Individuals can suffer from excessive debt. It can also limit their ability to achieve financial goals, such as saving for retirement or buying a home. In addition, excessive debt can lead to a downward spiral as individuals borrow more and more to make ends meet.

On a broader level, the American debt culture has negative consequences for the economy as a whole. High consumer debt can decrease spending, which lowers economic growth. It can also contribute to financial instability, as individuals and families struggle to pay off their debts and potentially default on their loans.

Despite the negative consequences of the American debt culture, there are steps individuals can take to break free from this cycle of debt. One of the most effective things anyone can do is create and stick to a budget. By tracking their income and expenses, individuals can better understand where their money is being spent and make informed decisions.

In addition, individuals can focus on paying down their debts, starting with the highest interest-rate deficits first. Make extra payments on these debts. Individuals can reduce interest over time and pay off their debts faster.

Individuals can change their mindset about money and possessions. By focusing on experiences and relationships rather than material possessions, individuals can find true happiness and fulfillment without relying on credit to fund their lifestyles.

How Real can it Get? What are Credit Statistics Saying?

According to the latest consumer debt data from the Federal Reserve Bank of New York, Americans' total credit card balance reached $986 billion in Q4 2022. This is the highest amount recorded since tracking began in 1999. This amount shows a $61 billion increase from the previous quarter, representing the most remarkable quarterly growth ever reported. In December 2022, the national average card debt among cardholders with unpaid balances was $7,279, including bank and retail credit cards.

The Stateless Millionaire Understands Debt, All the Way Through

Evidence of lending and borrowing can be traced back to ancient civilizations such as Mesopotamia and Egypt. Debt was often utilized to fund agricultural activities, which allowed farmers to acquire seeds, equipment, and labor.

Ancient Greece borrowed. The government often borrowed money from wealthy citizens to fund various expenses, including wars. Nevertheless, excessive borrowing ultimately led to a debt crisis in the fourth century BC, resulting in social unrest and radical political movements.

During the Middle Ages in Europe, the Catholic Church prohibited interest on loans. This gave rise to Jewish and Muslim moneylenders who provided credit at a cost. Debt was closely linked to trade and commerce growth as merchants and traders needed capital to finance their activities.

Banking and financial institutions have resulted in credit and debt expansion. The demand for credit to fund business expansion and investment in cutting-edge technologies was fueled by the Industrial Revolution and capitalism's rise. Middle classes have grown due to debt-fueled consumer spending.

Credit availability leads to debt crises and economic instability. This has been exemplified in several instances, including the Great Depression of the 1930s, the Asian financial crisis of the late 1990s, and the global financial crisis of 2008.

While acquiring credit may not necessarily be a negative move, it should only be considered in specific circumstances, for example, during an emergency with no other options. Debt should be used to finance capital projects likely to generate wealth rather than consumer goods. From my personal experience, I have come to understand that accumulating debt to sustain one's lifestyle without growth is not an effective method of amassing wealth. From a sustainable financial perspective, debt is justifiable if it is spent on an investment that brings returns.

6

Why Do You Want to Make Millions?

I stood on the edge of the bustling street, my heart racing as I scanned the horizon for a break in traffic. Cars zoomed past me in a blur, their engines roaring and horns blaring. I waited and waited and waited more, hoping for a chance to break from it.

Suddenly, the entire street erupted into chaos. Women in high heels darted past me, their feet pounding the pavement as they fled from an unseen threat. Without hesitation, I joined their frantic race to safety.

But my relief was short-lived. As I rounded the corner, I was confronted by a bully. He towered over me, sneering with contempt as he made me feel like the most petite person in the world. I could feel my face burning with shame as the other students looked on, watching me crumble under his taunts.

As an Iranian, I knew the consequences of weakness. My father was a proud and fierce man, and I feared the shame I would bring to my family if I admitted to being bullied. So I kept silent, suffering as the bully made my life hell.

Despite everything, I refused to let the bully win. I found joy in my friendships, even though my days were filled with dread and anxiety. But the bully's shadow hung over me, a constant reminder of fear and vulnerability beneath the surface of my daily routine.

Every day, I prayed for the strength to stand up to my tormentor, to show him that he couldn't break me. But he never relented, finding clever ways to enrage and humiliate me. Anger and frustration bubbled inside me like a volcano, threatening to explode at any moment.

That's when I turned to boxing. At first, it was just me and the walls of my room, my fists pounding against the plaster with a fury I didn't know I possessed. The first punch hurt like hell, my hand throbbing with pain, but I didn't stop. I closed my eyes and imagined the wall was my bully. With every strike, I felt a weight lift off my shoulders.

But it wasn't enough. I needed more. I sought out a boxing gym and began training in earnest. Every day, I pushed myself harder and harder until the sound of my gloves hitting the heavy bag echoed through the makeshift gym.

Then, one day, the moment I had been waiting for arrived. The bully tried to pick me up again, and this time, I was ready. I didn't hesitate. I lunged at him with all the ferocity I could muster, my fists flying like blurs. But he was taller and more powerful than me. Before I knew it, I was on the ground, my head spinning from the blow he had landed.

I wanted to give up. I wanted to crawl into a hole and never come out. But then I remembered why I started boxing in the first place. I picked myself up, my hands shaking with adrenaline, and faced the bully again. This time, I was ready for anything.

The reason behind our actions can often be just as crucial as the actions themselves. Why choose piles of money over booby traps and high heels? I knew exactly why I stood up to my bully: I was done with being a victim, tired of the constant humiliation, and didn't care about the consequences.

What're Your Motives?

But here's the thing: your motives could be half-baked, and that's where things get interesting. Sometimes, we act on impulse without fully understanding the reasons behind our actions. It's like running into a dark alleyway without knowing what's waiting for you on the other side. You might be driven by a burning desire for revenge or a fleeting moment of courage, but you're stumbling blindly into the unknown without a purpose.

This lack of understanding can be dangerous because we act without a clear direction or purpose. It's like navigating a ship without a compass - we might know where we want to go, but we don't know how to get there or what obstacles might lie in our path.

When our motives are half-baked, we are more vulnerable to making mistakes, taking risks we can't handle, or getting ourselves into dangerous situations. We might be driven by strong emotions like anger, fear, or excitement, but without a clear understanding of why we feel that way, we risk making impulsive decisions that we regret.

That's where self-reflection comes in. By taking the time to understand our motives and the reasons behind our actions, we can make more informed decisions and avoid getting ourselves into trouble. In other words, we must step back and ask ourselves why we want to do something.

The Stateless Millionaire knows Why

What if I told you that there's a millionaire out there who doesn't believe in the value of money itself? Meet the Stateless Millionaire, a person who understands the importance of money in our modern economies but also questions its purpose.

While money is undoubtedly a practical medium of exchange, it's not the only one out there. What if we used paper or diamonds instead? It's a fascinating question, especially since diamonds are often more valuable than paper money. But despite their worth, money remains the most practical and efficient transaction option.

Our beliefs about money and its purpose can significantly hinder our financial success. The Stateless Millionaire knows this firsthand. They grew up believing that money was only meant to satisfy their desires and needs. But as they gained more life experience, they realized money could be more.

Money can be a tool for achieving more ambitious goals and making a difference in the world. It's not just a means to an end but an invaluable resource that can help us achieve our dreams and create opportunities for ourselves and others.

Financial success isn't just about accumulating wealth. It's about understanding why you're doing it and being ready for whatever comes next. Just like the Stateless Millionaire, you need a clear sense of purpose and be prepared to take on any challenges that come your way because that's where the real adventure begins.

So step ahead, set those booby traps, sprint in your high heels, and stand up to your bullies. Just ensure you know why you're doing it, and be ready for whatever comes next. That's where the real adventure to becoming a Stateless Millionaire begins.

A Perspective on Money You Won't Find in Other Personal Finance Books

The term "energy" has become a buzzword in various contexts, from spirituality and chakras to expressing human beings' intangible qualities. This concept has gradually infiltrated western culture and is now a norm in our vocabulary. This leads to the question of how money can become a powerful force - energy.

Consider the scenario of an individual who has worked for five years in a regular eight-to-five job, with 52 working weeks and four weeks of holiday per year. In pursuing money, this person has spent approximately 10,000 hours of their life. Extending this to ten years of working experience, the individual has worked roughly 20,000 hours for money. If they continue to rely on a regular income to maintain a comfortable lifestyle, their physical and mental strength may last for another 50 to 60 years. To determine the total hours they will spend in their lifetime, multiply the remaining years by 2,000 hours.

This simple exercise intends to help you understand that money is a form of energy that requires time and effort. It may be physical, mental, or both. It doesn't matter why you want to earn money; the harsh truth is that if you're unclear on the "why," the "how" will be murky. At this point, you should settle the reasons for seeking money. The wrong "why" may result in you becoming a slave, working your entire life, and only receiving meager compensation from those who control you. In America, these "masters" may take on various guises such as employers, the healthcare system, or government programs.

The Stateless Millionaire Knows He's the Greatest Capital

The Stateless Millionaires see the hours they spend working for money as a part of themselves they cannot restore. They see themselves as their most lavish capital, and the money they earn is the return on that investment. They don't want to use their human capital until their energy runs out.

The concept of Stateless Millionaires is rooted in the idea that time is our most precious commodity. We should view ourselves as our greatest asset. These individuals understand that the hours they spend working for money are not something they can restore or regain once they've passed. As a result, they view their time and energy as limited resources that must be managed carefully to achieve the highest possible return on investment.

Stateless Millionaires strive for financial independence. They don't want to work for money indefinitely or use up valuable time and energy until they exhaust themselves. Instead, they seek to accumulate enough wealth to achieve freedom and autonomy.

7

Financial Discipline: Lessons Learned from Stock Market Investing.

It was a time when everything seemed to be going right. My business thrived, and I made more money than before. As a result, I indulged a bit, treating myself to the finer things in life. But more than that, I focused on the stock exchange market, particularly hedge funds.

I was captivated by the stories of the greats in the industry, legends like George Soros, who made over a billion dollars in a single day. The sheer audacity and skill required to achieve such a feat were awe-inspiring. I studied their every move, trying to learn from their success.

Every morning, I eagerly checked the stock exchange, looking for signs of movement that could impact my investments. I followed the news and watched global events, always looking for profit opportunities.

The adrenaline rush of watching the markets made me nuts. I made a couple of decisions without knowing what I was up against. My reasoning was against me. The stock exchange depicts real life. If you are not disciplined, you can't survive.

The All-too-Important Question

In one of my money workshops, a guy asked, "is financial discipline bully crap or an indulgence of the poor?"

"Are you married?" I asked him.

"Yes, I am," the guy replied.

"Do you have a kid?"

"Not yet."

"Suppose you have a three-year-old daughter who loves playing with sharp objects. Would you give her access to more dangerous objects?"

"No, I wouldn't," the guy said without a second thought.

"Do you have a driving license?"

"Yes, I do?"

"That's great. When I started driving, I enjoyed speeding through the countryside. After a severe accident with a heavy-duty truck that cost me thousands of dollars in repairs and medical bills, I learned it the difficult way. Do you know how many people die from carelessness on the road?"

"I don't know. I'd guess about 500,000."

"Every year, about 2 million people die from car crashes, with overspeeding, drunk driving, and falling asleep at the wheel being the primary causes," I said, adding, "what, is the leading cause of bankruptcy?"

"Medical issues."

"You got this one right."

"The most bizarre statistics according to a recent study show that 44.4% become bankrupt because they live above their means. How does this add up? Discipline is not just about restricting ourselves from harmful things; it's prioritizing our health and well-being. It's about cautioning ourselves in all aspects of our lives, including finance.

The Principle that Works for All

Successful people know how much they spend on essentials like housing, transportation, and clothing. They even keep track of small daily expenses like coffee and snacks from convenience stores!

Financial literacy and awareness are crucial for high net worth relative to income. On the other hand, those who struggle with their finances are often unaware of where their money is going. They may not realize how much they spend on small daily items and not keep track of expenses.

The difference between the two is staggering, highlighting the importance of paying attention to your expenses. By being mindful of your spending habits and making conscious choices about your expenditures, you can gain control of your finances. You can also work towards financial goals. So, if you're ready to take your finances to the next level, take a cue from successful millionaires and start tracking your expenses - you may be surprised at what you discover!

Why does it matter?

Your current earnings reflect your life so far. Additionally, small changes in your spending habits can accumulate over time and significantly impact your financial situation. Be mindful of your spending choices and improve them.

Whether you're trying to pay off debt, save for retirement, or reach other financial goals, discipline plays a crucial role in success.

One way to cultivate financial discipline is to create and stick to a budget. A budget helps you track your income and payments. This way, you know exactly how much money you have each month. It also helps prioritize your spending, so you can allocate your funds toward the things that matter most to you.

Another defining aspect of financial discipline is avoiding unnecessary expenses. This means resisting the temptation to splurge on things you don't need or can't afford, like expensive meals or luxury items. Instead, focus on living below your means and saving as much money as possible.

It's also crucial to be disciplined with debt management. This means making timely payments, avoiding taking on more debt than you can handle, and working towards paying off your debt as quickly as possible. By being disciplined with your debt, you can save money on interest payments and improve your credit score over time.

Most of us have heard how we need to be disciplined in our finances, but little has been said about discipline in investment.

Are you looking to become a successful investor? Then you need to master discipline! You can achieve your long-term financial goals with it. But what does it mean to be disciplined in investing? Let's break it down.

Firstly, you must develop a solid investment plan that aligns with your financial objectives, risk tolerance, and time horizon. This plan will serve as a roadmap to guide your investment decisions and help you stay on track.

But sticking to the plan is easier said than done. That's where discipline comes in. You must resist the temptation to follow the crowd, chase the latest investment fad, or panic during market volatility. A disciplined investor will remain focused on their long-term goals without being distracted by short-term market noise.

Regular portfolio reviews ensure it aligns with your investment plan. You may need to adjust, but a disciplined investor won't change market fluctuations radically.

Diversification is another arm of discipline. Investing in different asset classes, sectors, and locations can reduce risk and capture long-term growth opportunities. Disciplined investors have a well-diversified portfolio aligned with their investment plan.

Successful investing is not a sprint; it's a marathon. A disciplined investor understands this and will not be tempted to make impulsive decisions in response to short-term market movements. They know that achieving long-term financial goals requires a steady and consistent approach.

So, if you want to become a successful investor, make discipline your best friend!

Part Two

Taking Action

"Don't watch the clock; do what it does. Keep going." - Sam Levenson

8

Money Moves towards People in Motion

The sun blazed overhead as I looked at my humble plot of land, just a few acres in size. It was a daunting sight. With a small team of friends whom I convinced to become partners, I set out to create an agro-business. This would provide a means of fleeing the country.

From the get-go, I knew I needed to invest in the right technology and choose crops in high demand. But we didn't have enough money. We labored in the fields, facing hurdle after hurdle, from pests and diseases to bureaucracy and market fluctuations.

The business blossomed. I formed partnerships with local supermarkets and restaurants. They marveled at the crispness of my cucumbers, the juiciness of my tomatoes, and the fiery flavor of my peppers. And as word of mouth spread, my business grew beyond what I could have imagined.

Looking back on my journey, I am proud of what my friends and I have accomplished. We made a move.

It was Time to Act

So, once I finished my shift, I rushed home and crafted a plan for my life. I outlined how I wanted to live and the level of independence I desired. Time passed, the seasons changed, and I found myself still at my job, feeling like I was wasting my potential. I decided it was time to act. I enrolled in night school.

I focused on web development, graphic design, and digital marketing. Although the coursework was rigorous, I was determined to learn as much as possible. I spent hours practicing coding, designing graphics, and studying various digital marketing strategies.

As I progressed, my confidence and enthusiasm grew. I saw the potential of my new skills and how they could benefit my career. Web development piqued my interest, so I spent considerable time honing my coding skills and building websites. I even created a portfolio of my work to showcase to potential employers.

After several job interviews, I landed a web developer position at a small start-up. I was thrilled to be allowed to apply my new skills and work alongside the company's founders to build and maintain their website.

The Stateless Millionaire Makes Money Moves

Picture this: a millionaire with no fixed address, no nationality, and no restrictions on where they can go. How did they amass such wealth? Understanding a fundamental finance principle: "Money Moves towards People in Motion."

The stateless millionaire knows that being proactive and taking action toward your financial goals can lead to financial success. They understand that simply having money isn't enough; it's about taking the initiative to create opportunities that bring money in.

Successful entrepreneurs and investors are prime examples of this principle in action. They are always on the move, seeking new opportunities and taking action to make their dreams a reality. They attract investors, customers, and partners who invest their money in their business ventures.

The stateless millionaire recognizes that investing in assets that appreciate or saving for retirement can attract monetary resources to yourself. They understand that financial success isn't just about having money but about taking action toward your economic goals.

9

The Stateless Millionaire Gives Back

I was designing an e-commerce website for a client in Canada who sold jewelry when I decided to take a coffee break. I walked to the nearby café and ordered a latte, sitting by the window to enjoy the view outside. As I sipped my coffee, my mind wandered back to website design. I mulled over the different options.

As I gazed out the window, I noticed a group of people across the street. They were gathered around a street performer who was playing guitar and singing. The music was beautiful, and I tapped my foot into the rhythm.

Suddenly, a man appeared beside me, interrupting my reverie. "Excuse me, Ma," he said. "Do you have a minute to discuss our charity?"

I looked up at him, taken aback. He was wearing a brightly colored T-shirt with a local charity logo emblazoned on it. "Sure," I said, intrigued. "What's your charity about?"

The man explained the charity's mission of providing clean water to rural communities in developing countries. I listened attentively, nodding and asking questions.

As he spoke, I became more interested in the charity's work. "That sounds amazing," I said. "How can I help?"

The man grinned, pulling out a clipboard. "Well, you can sign up to volunteer at our next event or donate right here." He pointed to a stack of flyers on the table beside him.

I hesitated, feeling torn. On the one hand, I was eager to return to work on the e-commerce site. Meanwhile, I felt a strong urge to contribute to society and do some good.

I decided to make a small donation, grateful for the opportunity to contribute to a worthy cause.

Over the years, I have been more intentional about giving and plan to give continuously. I do this because I understand that giving is one of the universal laws of nature. It is the responsibility of the Stateless Millionaire to give back.

Take Mo Ibrahim, for instance. He's a Sudanese-British entrepreneur and billionaire who has used his wealth to create the Mo Ibrahim Foundation. This organization promotes good governance and leadership in Africa and even awards the Mo Ibrahim Prize for Achievement in African Leadership. This award recognizes former African heads of state who have shown exceptional leadership and contributed significantly to their country's development.

Another inspiring example is Patrick Soon-Shiong. He's a South African-American surgeon, entrepreneur, and philanthropist who's using his wealth to fund cancer research and develop new treatments for the disease. He's even created the Chan Soon-Shiong Institute of Molecular Medicine, which focuses on personalized medicine and using a patient's genetic profile to create tailored treatments.

These stateless millionaires understand that with great power comes great responsibility, and they've made it their mission to give back to humanity in meaningful ways. They're using their wealth and resources to make a positive impact and improve the lives of others. It just goes to show that wealth isn't just a symbol of success, but also a powerful tool that can be used for the greater good.

It's Can't Get Simpler

I never expected my brief encounter with a charity worker to leave a lasting impact on me. But it did. The most beautiful part of life is giving back to society and contributing to something greater than myself. Stateless Millionaires leverage their wealth and resources to make a positive impact, inspiring others to follow in their footsteps. The greatest wealth one can possess is not material possessions but the ability to create a meaningful difference in the world. So, I plan to do my part and contribute to society in any way possible, whether through donations or volunteer work. Because at the end of the day, we're not just here to accumulate wealth and success but to positively affect the world around us.

10

Is it Wrong to Keep Money Aside for Sunny Days

"Ali, you see this hole? It can help you when the rain is heavy," I was told. It became part of me to save even the tiniest amount of money I could, putting it into my little piggy bank. My parents instilled in me the value of saving and how it could help me in the long run.

My parents' story about a small hole in the ground is a thriller. They explained that during heavy rain, the hole would serve as a lifesaver, collecting water we could use in the future. But that wasn't the only lesson they taught me. They also instilled in me the value of saving money, no matter how small the amount.

And as I grew older, that lesson became even more profound.

I Know Better

I was taught savings were for rainy days when everything is bleak. While this is not a terrible idea, it certainly won't work at this age and time. Do you know why? Any money you save, whether in a piggy or traditional bank, is subject to inflation. This means its value will decrease over time due to rising goods and services costs.

Let's say you have $100 in a savings account at 1% interest per year, and the inflation rate is 2% yearly.

After one year, your savings account will have earned $1 in interest, bringing your total balance to $101. But due to inflation, the cost of goods and services has also increased by 2%, so your purchasing power has decreased.

In other words, your $101 can now only buy the same goods and services that $98 could buy the year before.

If this trend continues, your savings will lose value and may not be enough to cover your future expenses.

I wish I could travel back in time and tell those piggy bankers how wrong they were. "Hey, you were wrong!" You do not save for rainy days. You save for sunny days because we have more of them in a year.

The Eight Myths About Saving

Saving money is a valuable financial habit that can help you achieve your monetary goals and prepare for unexpected expenses. The truth is that many myths about saving keep you from achieving your financial goals. Here are eight common saving myths you should know. The first is the real deal:

1. "We save because of unseen expenses." Nope, we don't. We save for the future. If you want to keep money aside for unseen expenses, it's a different ball game, and I advise you to have a contingency fund.

2. "I don't earn enough to save." This misconception can hold you back from building a healthy savings account. Even if you only save a small

amount each month, it can add up over time and help you reach your financial goals.

3. "I can't save and still enjoy my life." Saving doesn't mean you have to live a deprivation-filled life. You can still enjoy your hobbies while saving money. The key is to prioritize your spending and find a balance between your short-term and long-term financial goals.

4. "I'll start saving when I make more money." Waiting until you make more money to begin saving is a mistake. The earlier you start, the more time your money has to grow and accumulate interest.

5. "I don't need to save because I have a good job." No matter how lucrative your job is, it's imperative to have a safety net in case of unexpected expenses or job loss. Saving can help you prepare for these situations and give you peace of mind.

6. "I'll rely on credit cards if I need money." Relying on credit cards to cover unexpected expenses can lead to high-interest rates and debt. A healthy savings account can help you avoid this situation and give you more financial security.

7. "I don't need to save for retirement yet." It's never too early to start saving for retirement. The earlier you start, the more time your money has to grow and accumulate compound interest.

8. "I can't save because I have too much debt." While it's essential to pay off your debt, it's also worthwhile to save at the same time. Even if you only

save a small amount each month, it can add up over time and help you achieve your financial goals.

Savings prioritize your future over short-term expenses.

When you prioritize saving money, you commit to your future financial well-being. By putting money aside for the future, you prioritize your long-term financial goals over short-term expenses.

While it may be tempting to spend money on immediate wants and needs, such as the latest tech gadget or a night out with friends, consider the impact of these expenses on your long-term financial health. If you constantly spend your money on immediate gratification, you may struggle to pay for unexpected expenditures or save for future goals. For example, acquiring a home or saving for retirement.

Prioritizing savings helps you develop valuable skills. Saving money requires thinking about your spending and making intentional decisions about your financial priorities. Over time, this can help you build a solid monetary foundation that supports you in achieving your long-term economic goals.

When you save money, you build a financial cushion for unexpected expenses and set yourself up for success when opportunities arise. This is because having savings gives you the freedom and flexibility to take advantage of opportunities as they come up, without worrying about where the money will come from.

For example, let's say you've always dreamed of starting your own business but never had the financial resources. However, if you've saved money consistently, you may be better positioned to pursue your dream when the opportunity arises. You may be able to use your savings to invest in your business or to cover your living expenses while you get your business off the ground.

Similarly, if you come across an opportunity to invest in a promising stock or real estate property, having savings can give you the financial flexibility to take advantage of the opportunity without borrowing money or dipping into your emergency fund.

When you save money, you are better positioned to take action when opportunities arise, whether it's starting a business, investing in your education, or pursuing your dream career. Saving gives you the financial freedom and flexibility to take advantage of opportunities and achieve your long-term financial goals.

When times get tough, don't depend on savings to cover expenses or splurge on luxury items.

The Stateless Millionaire Saves and Use it Wisely

The Stateless Millionaire knows that saving money isn't just a means of survival - it's a way to pay themselves and open up new avenues for future investments.

While some may view saving as a sacrifice or restriction on spending habits, the Stateless Millionaire sees it as a powerful tool for financial growth. By consistently keeping a portion of their income, they create a safety net for themselves while setting aside funds for future investment opportunities.

Rather than relying on their savings as a last resort, the Stateless Millionaire views them as a means of achieving their long-term financial goals. They understand that carefully managing their finances and consistently saving can create a secure foundation for their wealth to grow.

So forget about living paycheck to paycheck or relying on credit to cover expenses - follow in the footsteps of the Stateless Millionaire and start saving for your future financial success.

11

Stateless Millionaires Leverage Financial System

My first big question when I entered the real estate world was, "how do I finance my first property?"

I had some savings, but it wasn't enough to cover the entire cost of the property I had my eye on. I knew I needed to find a way to secure additional funds, so I decided to look into loans.

After crunching the numbers and comparing different lenders, I realized this particular lender had the most competitive interest rates and repayment terms. With their loan, I secured the necessary funds to purchase the property I had my eye on. I was nervous as I filled out the application and gathered all the required documents, including my income statements, credit history, and employment information. But the lender was a gem and guided me through each step of the application process.

To my relief, I received the news that my application had been approved! The loan covered the majority of the property purchase price. The lender helped me acquire the property, and I finally took my first step toward building my real estate portfolio.

What Banks and Big Companies Like Apple Don't Want you to know About Loans

Let's talk about loans, a financial tool many people and businesses rely on to finance big-ticket items or investments. But here's another secret that banks and big companies like Apple don't want you to know: loans can come with hidden fees and sky-high interest rates that can blow your budget out of the water.

When taking out a loan, interest rate is one of the most critical factors to watch out for. Sure, banks and other lenders may lure you in with low-interest rates, but beware! These rates can shoot up quickly, especially if you miss payments or your credit score takes a dip. This means that you could end up shelling out way more in interest over the life of the loan than you initially bargained for.

In addition to high-interest rates, many loans have hidden fees that can add up quickly. For example, some lenders charge origination fees, which are a percentage of the total loan amount. In addition, they charge processing fees, which cover underwriting costs. These fees can add hundreds or even thousands of dollars to the loan cost, making it much more expensive than you anticipated.

Banks and big companies like Apple also don't want you to know that there are alternatives to traditional loans, such as peer-to-peer lending and crowdfunding. These platforms allow borrowers to connect directly with individual investors who lend money at competitive rates. This is ideal for those looking for a more transparent and affordable loan option.

Do your research and read the fine print before taking out any loan. Don't be swayed by low-interest rates or promises of easy approval – ensure you understand all of the terms and fees associated with the loan before signing on the dotted line.

Mortgage and Commercial Loan

If you're looking for a loan, you may have heard the terms "mortgage" and "commercial loan" thrown around. But what's the difference between the two? Let's break it down.

A mortgage is a loan used to purchase a property, such as a house or a condo. It's a long-term loan paid back over 10 to 30 years, and the property is collateral. If you default on the loan, the lender can seize the property to recoup their losses. The interest rate on a mortgage is usually fixed, meaning it won't change over the repayment period.

Commercial loans support businesses in achieving their goals, whether it's purchasing equipment, inventory, or acquiring commercial property.

Commercial loans are different from mortgages because they are not necessarily secured by a property. Instead, the lender considers the business's financial health and the borrower's creditworthiness to approve the loan. Repayment terms vary from a few months to several years, with fixed or variable interest rates. If you want to grow your business, a commercial loan is ideal. If you're buying a home, a mortgage is better. Knowing these differences will help you choose the right loan for your financial goals.

The bottom line

Loans can be a double-edged sword - on the one hand, they can help you achieve your financial dreams, but on the other, they can plunge you into a never-ending cycle of debt. To ensure you use loans to your advantage, you must do your due diligence and make informed decisions.

Before taking out a loan, do your homework and carefully consider the terms and conditions. Think about interest rates, fees, and repayment terms and ensure you can afford monthly payments. Don't forget to have a solid plan for paying back the loan. This includes budgeting and avoiding debt that you can handle.

The truth is, loans can be a powerful financial tool, but only when used responsibly. By taking a thoughtful approach and making informed decisions, you can leverage loans to achieve your financial goals and create a brighter economic future.

12

Adapting to Changes

I used to drag myself to Walmart or any store within reach whenever I needed something. But today, everything has changed dramatically. The emergence of online shopping and e-commerce has opened up a whole new world of possibilities for me as a consumer. I can now effortlessly explore numerous options, compare prices, scrutinize reviews, and buy anything I want, all from home. Technology has revolutionized how we shop and engage with products, and it's astonishing.

Gone are the days of trudging through crowded stores, battling long checkout lines, and feeling lost among endless rows of merchandise. Online shopping has transformed traditional shopping. With the rise of e-commerce, I can now explore an almost infinite number of products from countless vendors worldwide without leaving my home.

Traditional work models are changing dramatically as remote work becomes more prevalent, blurring the lines between work and personal life. This transformation has given rise to creative and analytical jobs that require critical thinking and problem-solving skills.

Businesses adapt by becoming more efficient and reducing large workforces. The emergence of digital marketing and e-commerce has opened up new opportunities for growth and expansion, allowing companies to reach a wider audience. However, these changes come with new challenges, such as maintaining a work-life balance and the need for upskilling and reskilling.

We must embrace and adapt to these changes to thrive in this exciting age of possibility. Failing to adapt can cost companies their existence, as seen with Kodak and Blockbuster.

As we advance, we must realize that many jobs will become obsolete within a few decades due to technological advancements. This may sound daunting, but it's an opportunity to adapt and move. Those with access to information who know how to use it to their advantage will come out on top.

As an information age product, I can attest to the power of investing in yourself. This includes staying current with the latest trends and technologies, networking with other entrepreneurs, and attending conferences and workshops. By embracing change and being willing to take risks, you can grow beyond what you imagined possible.

The information age is not a threat but an opportunity. Seize it and make the most of it by investing in your education, staying up-to-date with the latest technologies and trends, connecting with like-minded individuals, and being willing to take risks and embrace change.

The Stateless Millionaire is Adaptative

The stateless millionaire understands innovation's power and stays ahead of the curve. Yesterday's strategies may not work today. Whether it's exploring new industries or developing new skills, they're always looking for ways to stay ahead of the game.

But being a stateless millionaire isn't just about adaptability; it's also about taking calculated risks. They know that with change comes uncertainty, and failure is often a necessary step toward success. They're willing to experiment with new ideas, pivot quickly if something isn't working, and take risks to achieve their goals.

What sets stateless millionaires apart is their ability to reinvent themselves constantly. They don't let tradition or old ways of thinking hold them back; they challenge assumptions and are open to new perspectives. They are true masters of their destiny, shaping their lives and businesses to utilize the world's ever-changing landscape.

In a world where the only constant changes, the stateless millionaire is a shining example of what can be achieved by embracing adaptability, innovation, and risk-taking.

12

The Stateless Millionaire Creates Value at Every Turn

When I landed my first job, I was like a kid in a candy store. I couldn't wait to start working and prove my worth. It was a humble beginning, cleaning floors and taking out the trash, but I was ready to take on any task. But, as the days turned into weeks and the weeks turned into months, I realized that the work was far from glamorous. It was monotonous, and the tasks were never-ending. But I persevered, working tirelessly between shifts and adding more jobs to my busy schedule.

As a diligent worker, I thought I created value. After all, my job was to keep the environment clean and tidy. But over time, I realized value creation was more than working hard. It was about understanding the customer's needs and exceeding their expectations.

I learned that being a value creator meant taking ownership of my work, thinking creatively, and finding ways to improve existing processes and systems. I was no longer content with doing what I was told or following instructions. I began to take a more strategic approach to my work, always looking for ways to add value and make a difference.

As an entrepreneur, I prioritize value creation. I understand that to succeed in today's fast-paced and ever-changing business world, I must constantly seek feedback from my customers and use that feedback to improve my products and services. I invest in my education and stay up-to-date with the latest trends and technologies. This is so I can offer my customers the best value.

Creating value requires a willingness to take risks, think outside the box, and constantly look for creative opportunities. As I continue my entrepreneurial journey, I will always keep value creation at the forefront of everything I do.

What is Value Creation

It's a term frequently thrown around in the business world. But what does it mean? And why is it so critical?

Value creation is about improving things. It's about improving existing products, services, or processes to make them more valuable to customers. This can be done in a variety of ways - by reducing costs, enhancing quality, increasing convenience, or adding new features, to name just a few examples.

But why is value creation so important? The answer is simple: in today's competitive environment, people that don't create value are unlikely to survive. Customers and employers have more choices than ever and are increasingly sophisticated in purchasing decisions. They want products and services that meet their needs and exceed their expectations and are willing to pay a premium for those that do.

Starting up a business is a risky proposition, and the odds of success are stacked against you. But by focusing on creating value for your customers, you can increase your chances of success. When you offer something truly valuable, customers will choose your product or service over your competitors. And as you continue to create value, you can build a loyal customer base that will sustain your business over the long term.

Of course, creating value is also for employees. The more value you create, the more you are rewarded. But it's easier said than done. It requires a deep understanding of your customer's needs and preferences and a willingness to take risks and try new things. But with the right mindset and approach, value creation can be a powerful tool for business success. So the next time you hear "value creation," remember that it's not just a buzzword - it's the key to building a successful business in today's fast-paced, ever-changing world.

Step 1: Identify a product or service you are currently offering or planning to offer.

Step 2: Think about the target market for this product or service. Who are they, what needs and wants, and what problems are they trying to solve?

Step 3: Brainstorm a list of ways to add value to your product or service to better meet your target market's needs. This could include adding new features, improving the design, offering better customer support, or providing additional resources or tools.

Step 4: Prioritize your list based on the impact each idea would have on your target market and the feasibility of implementing it.

Step 5: Choose one or two of the most impactful and feasible ideas and create a plan to implement them.

Step 6: Launch your updated product or service and gather feedback from your customers. Use this feedback to continue improving and adding value over time.

This exercise can help you think more deeply about your customers' needs and how you can better meet them through value creation. It can also help you stay ahead of the competition and grow your business."

Stateless millionaires choose excellence.

I started my web development and online marketing business out of my passion for developing innovative solutions for businesses. When I started, I believed taking shortcuts and looking for quick fixes would be the best approach. However, as I learned more about the industry and worked with clients, I quickly realized that excellence was the only way to achieve long-term success.

I made it my mission to embrace excellence in everything I did. I started by prioritizing continuous learning and development. I researched new technologies, best practices, and industry trends. I also invested in myself by attending webinars, conferences, and workshops to improve my skills and knowledge.

I also focused on delivering exceptional service to my clients. I understood that my success was directly tied to their success, and I made it a duty to understand their business goals and tailor my solutions to meet their unique needs. I would go above and beyond to ensure their websites were user-friendly, visually appealing, and optimized for search engines. I also provided ongoing support to ensure their websites performed well and met their business goals.

To achieve excellence, I also embrace a growth mindset. I see every challenge and setback as an opportunity for learning and improvement. I constantly ask for feedback from my clients and implement their suggestions to improve my services. I also seek mentors and industry experts to learn from their experiences and gain new insights.

As a stateless individual who has succeeded against all odds, I used to believe that the quickest and easiest way to reach my goals was the best approach. However, my journey has taught me that taking shortcuts and looking for quick fixes can only lead to short-term gains and mediocrity. Unfortunately, many people still hold onto this belief, not realizing that it's a dangerous mindset that's not suitable for stateless millionaires who pursue long-term success and impact.

Do you think you can do much without being excellent?

For every stateless millionaire, excellence must be ingrained as a fundamental principle. It's an understanding that success is not a destination, but a journey that requires constant improvement. In other words, excellence is a way of life. It's a mindset that drives stateless millionaires to strive for the best in every aspect of their lives.

Stateless millionaires know that hard work and perseverance are necessary to succeed long-term. They don't look for quick fixes or shortcuts. They know that success is not just about achieving a specific goal or reaching a certain level of success. It's a continuous journey that requires constant resilience and perseverance in the face of challenges and setbacks.

To achieve excellence, stateless millionaires adopt a growth mindset. They embrace challenges and failures as opportunities for learning and development and use them to improve their skills and knowledge. They are constantly pushing themselves to be better, not just for personal gain, but also to make a positive impact on the world around them.

Excellence Means Soft Skills Also.

Excellence in any field requires a range of skills beyond technical expertise. These skills are commonly referred to as soft skills and they are essential for individuals who want to excel in their professional lives.

Soft skills are a set of personal attributes, communication abilities, and social graces that allow individuals to interact effectively with others. They include skills such as teamwork, communication, leadership, adaptability, problem-solving, and time management. These skills are not innate but can be developed and improved with practice.

Soft skills are relevant in today's fast-paced and competitive job market. Employers are not only looking for candidates with technical know-how, but also those with strong communication skills, the ability to work well in a team, and the ability to solve problems creatively.

For instance, in the workplace, individuals with excellent communication skills can convey their ideas and viewpoints to their colleagues and clients, ensuring that their message is understood and valued.

Effective communication also fosters better relationships with team members and stakeholders, which can lead to improved collaboration and productivity.

Leadership is another vital soft skill valued in the workplace. It enables individuals to inspire, motivate and guide their team members toward achieving a common goal. Effective leaders delegate tasks but also provide direction, and support, and take responsibility for their team's actions.

Excellence also refers to the ability to adapt to changing situations and challenges. In today's rapidly evolving world, change is constant, and individuals who can adapt and learn quickly have a competitive edge. Adaptability allows individuals to stay ahead of the curve, develop innovative solutions, and respond to challenges with resilience and agility.

14

The power of Focus

My friend and I just finished a weekend class. We both thought, "Why not?" Let's go out to the woods to hunt." I felt like galloping off. I've learned how to fight, withstand a bully, and show him what I got. My shooting skills are great. My friend is a pro.

We packed our bags with hunting gear and set out. I felt alive. We soon reached our destination and began to set up camp. To grasp what we were up against, we explored the area, looking for signs of wildlife. The thrill of being in the wild was undeniable.

Sure, some may question why we were out there. For me, it was another opportunity to challenge myself and push my limits. I've always believed in being prepared for whatever life throws my way.

And with my friend by my side, a seasoned hunter, I knew I was in good hands. As we walked, he shared tips and tricks. His knowledge and experience were valuable assets to our expedition.

"What's your greatest challenge hunting?" I asked

"It's keeping an eye on the game," my friend said. "I watch the target, always. I don't care who's screaming or laughing. My eyes don't go off."

"What if you come across a park?" I asked.

"It doesn't change a thing. I fix my eyes on a target. When it's down, I go for another and then another."

We conversed as we ventured out of the camp and into the dense woods. Our chatter stopped as my companion stepped forward, signaling a stop. I hit the red button - literally - and stopped my track. I didn't move a muscle until my friend did.

Together, we moved cautiously, making minimal noise as we traversed the forest floor. Every step we took was measured and deliberate as we attempted to blend in with the surrounding environment.

Then I saw a magnificent bear wandering around in the woods, seemingly without a care in the world. The creature's size and stature commanded respect, and its presence sent shivers down my spine.

As I gazed in awe at the magnificent creature, my mind was transported to the days of King Logan- the ancient ruler known for his strength and power. The bear walked with the same majestic aura as the fabled king. This caused me to feel reverence and admiration for this wild animal.

"Take a shot," my friend said.

My pulse quickened as I raised my rifle, adrenaline pumping through my veins. This was my moment. A rush of confidence surged through me as I aimed at the massive bear before me. "Trust me, baby," I told myself. "I've got this."

I pulled the trigger, but my shot veered wildly off course. The bear fled into the forest, leaving me deflated. "That was not even close," I muttered under my breath.

I steadied my grip and fired again. The seconds ticked by agonizingly slowly as I waited for the shot to land. And then, it happened. The bear fell to the ground, its massive body thudding against the earth. A wave of triumph washed over me. I took down a bear.

Taking the Shot Thereafter

In my career, I was convinced I could effortlessly slip into any coat and maintain my composure. I believed I could do anything as long as it was legal. Being trained as a doctor with a knack for marketing and selling is exhilarating. People called me multi-talented. Honestly, it was easy to see why. You might even doubt that I could possess all these abilities, but I assure you, I did.

I craved more, wanted to become all I could be, and believed nothing could stop me. Let me be clear; I didn't acquire all these skills overnight. As I mentioned in an earlier chapter of this book, I was a farmer in Iran, despite having only an average education. When I moved to the United States, I had to work several menial jobs for six months to make ends meet. I then got my doctorate in neurology.

Now, you might think that someone like me, with such diverse skill sets, could do just about anything, right? After all, I only have one life to live and want to make the most of it. But let me tell you what I've discovered.

You Can't Do Everything.

Life is a never-ending episode filled with opportunities and possibilities. But there's a catch: we all have limited resources. Each day, we wake up with the same amount of time and energy, and it's up to us to choose how to utilize it. The world champions multitasking and productivity, making it easy to fall prey to the temptation of accomplishing everything. But the truth is, life is all about focus, and you can't do it all.

The ability to focus begins with a clear sense of direction and purpose. It means recognizing what matters to you and putting your time and energy into achieving them. It means being mindful of what you say yes and no to. With a focus, you can make decisions that align with your values and objectives. You're less likely to be sidetracked by things that are not a priority.

Trying to do everything leads to chaos and unfulfillment. If you attempt to do it all, you stretch yourself too thin, and you won't be able to give anything your full attention or effort. You'll become a jack of all trades but a master of none. You'll also be under constant stress and overwhelmed, struggling to keep up with the endless list of tasks and commitments.

Have a Target in Your Work and Business. It Saves the Stress of Pursuing What's Not

When it comes to work or business, having a clear goal can mean the difference between success and floundering in a sea of unattainable objectives. Without a target in sight, it's easy to get lost in the hustle and bustle of daily life. You chase after any shiny object that comes your way without any real sense of direction or purpose.

But when you have a well-defined target in your sights, everything changes. Suddenly, you know exactly what you're working towards. You can break it down into specific goals and checkpoints to track your progress. You become a decision-making ninja, evaluating every opportunity and task based on whether or not it aligns with your ultimate objective. If it doesn't, you toss it aside and focus on what matters.

Not only does having a target help you prioritize and manage your time, energy, and resources, and also provides an anchor in rough waters. You can concentrate your efforts on the tasks and projects that are most meaningful and directly contribute to achieving your goal while letting less critical duties fall by the wayside. And when the going gets tough, you can use the progress made towards your target as a beacon of hope and motivation to keep you moving forward, no matter what obstacles you encounter.

Multi-tasking

It's impressive to see people who can juggle multiple tasks at once - talking on the phone with friends while cooking dinner and chasing after their kids. But while multitasking may seem like a clever way to be productive, it can negatively affect performance and overall well-being.

Studies have found that when people try to focus on multiple tasks simultaneously, their attention becomes divided, resulting in decreased effectiveness and efficiency. So, even though they finish several jobs, their quality may be subpar. It may take them longer to complete everything than if they concentrated on one task at a time.

Multitasking triggers stress and burnout. When people constantly switch between tasks, they don't give their brains a chance to rest and rejuvenate. This can lead to increased exhaustion and overwhelm.

As someone who has gone through the ebbs and flows of the working world, I know firsthand that settling for less is never the answer. Nobody deserves to stay stuck in a low-paying job or hit a career plateau without a way out. Sometimes, taking on multiple jobs is the only way to make ends meet and achieve financial stability.

But here's the catch: taking on multiple jobs doesn't mean doing them all. That's a recipe for disaster and leads to decreased productivity and burnout. To truly succeed in juggling numerous jobs, effective time management is crucial. It's essential to prioritize tasks and set boundaries to ensure each job receives the attention it deserves.

The Stateless Millionaire is Focused

Imagine living your dream life despite the global economy's twists and turns. That's the reality for a stateless millionaire - someone who has achieved financial independence by diversifying their income streams and investments across different markets and sectors.

Stateless millionaires create financial safety nets that protect them from geopolitical uncertainty. But it takes more than multitasking to reach this level of success.

A stateless millionaire has a laser focus on their long-term goals. This means evaluating every opportunity that comes your way and only pursuing those that align with your vision. Shiny objects and short-term gains won't distract you from your priorities.

By staying true to your strategy and priorities, you can create a diversified portfolio that protects your wealth and maximizes your earning potential. Being a stateless millionaire is the ultimate achievement in financial independence. It requires a clear understanding of what truly matters to you.

15

Diversification

The bell rang, signaling my departure from the café. But as I steered through the crowd, I caught sight of a striking figure. It was a guy from one of the Arabian countries. Rumor had it that he was a prince with so much wealth that he could buy and sell entire cities.

As he strolled by in one of his many Lamborghinis, I watched him from afar, each car more extravagant than the last. To me, he was a god among mortals - untouchable, unapproachable.

But then, an idea struck me. I turned to my friend and told him I would invite this prince for a coffee. My friend scoffed, telling me that my measly weekly salary couldn't even buy a cup of coffee for this guy.

But I refused to be intimidated. I shrugged my shoulders and smiled mischievously, determined to take a risk.

As I approached him, my heart pounding with excitement and nerves, I tried to keep my cool. I summoned the courage to ask him if he wanted to join me for coffee. I hoped he wouldn't see through my actions.

To my surprise, he smiled and agreed. We went to a nearby café, and I couldn't believe my luck. As we sat down, I struggled to find the right words, trying to make a positive impression on this mysterious, wealthy man.

But as we talked, I realized he was just like anyone else. The way he spoke to me was genuine, and he was interested in learning about my struggles and dreams.

As the conversation flowed, I relaxed and opened up to him. I shared my aspirations and fears, and he listened intently, offering encouragement and advice.

I told him what I had in mind - to build him a personal website to highlight his wealth and seal his reputation as the most famous person on campus. Did he buy into the idea? No, he didn't, and I didn't get my money back either.

Fear or Gain: Which Comes First?

Investing your hard-earned money is not fun, especially when you're looking to secure your financial future. And while many people think they've got it all figured out, most end up shooting themselves in the foot.

I've seen it happen time and time again. People save for years or inherit a large sum of money, and they're so afraid of losing it that they don't know what to do with it. They end up with a wallet full of holes or a bank account that isn't growing.

But the desire to make your money work for you is normal. The problem is that most people don't understand diversification.

Putting all your savings into one investment opportunity may seem like a brilliant idea, but it's a recipe for disaster. Even the most promising investments can fail, leaving you with nothing.

That's why diversification is crucial. By spreading your savings across different investment opportunities, you minimize your risk and increase your chances of success.

Of course, diversification isn't just about throwing your money at any investment opportunity that comes your way. Do your research and carefully consider your financial goals and risk tolerance.

But when done right, diversification can be the key to financial stability and growth. It's a strategy successful investors and financial experts swear by.

Diversification shouldn't be limited to multiple employment positions. Anyone looking to achieve financial freedom must consider all available income sources. Investing in stocks and real estate and starting a business requires diversification to ensure long-term stability. Increasing earning potential and mitigating risk can be achieved by diversifying income sources. This provides freedom to pursue other opportunities and work towards life goals.

Helpful Tips on Diversifying I learned

I learned this the difficult way through my financial mistakes, but I've gained some helpful diversification tips I want to share with you. The first step is to understand your financial goals and risk tolerance. You can't achieve your objectives if you don't know what they are. Reflect on what you hope to accomplish with your investments and how much risk you're comfortable taking.

Don't limit yourself to one type of investment once you understand your goals and risk tolerance. Research and consider several options, from stocks and bonds to real estate and even alternative buys like cryptocurrency. Diversifying across different industries and sectors can also minimize risk.

But don't just set it and forget it! Regularly reviewing and adjusting your investments is essential to ensure you stay on track to meet your goals and minimize risk. As your goals and risk tolerance change, so should your investment strategy.

Finally, don't be afraid to seek professional advice. A financial advisor can help you navigate market conditions and create a personalized investment portfolio tailored to your goals and risk tolerance.

I have achieved financial stability by following these tips. So can you!

Diversification is not just some fancy strategy reserved for elites. Stateless millionaires benefit from this concept to protect their finances and achieve financial goals. The hard truth is: money can be unpredictable, and even the most financially savvy individuals can fall victim to unforeseen losses.

The Stateless Millionaire is Diverse

But with diversification, you have the power to spread your investments across a wide range of options, reducing the risk of losing everything if one investment fails. It also allows you to capitalize on opportunities for growth in various industries and sectors, increasing your chances of success.

Diversification shields your finances from risks and helps you achieve long-term financial growth. You won't solely rely on one investment to perform well to make a profit if you invest in several options. Even if one investment underperforms, the others can make up for it, and you can still see a positive return overall.

Therefore, regardless of your financial status, diversification is a strategy to consider. It can help you grow your money, protect your funds, and achieve financial stability and success.

16

Finding the Land of Opportunity

For weeks, I've observed a man who stood out from the crowd on a busy avenue. He wore a suit and tie and carried a briefcase wherever he was. But what caught my attention was the group of people he surrounded himself with - people who struggled to make ends meet, who didn't have a penny to spare for groceries or laundry, let alone appreciate art or music.

Yet there he was, sharing his paintings with them, explaining the intricacies of each brushstroke and color used. I couldn't help but wonder why he bothered with such an audience.

One day, I decided to approach him and find out. As I got closer, I saw him showing a painting to a woman with a cane and a worn-out coat. The man explained the picture to her, and when he finished, she looked up at him with a smile. She said, "Thank you, young man. But I still don't know how useful this is to me."

It was then that I knew I had to talk to him. I introduced myself and asked him about his art and his motivation for sharing it with people who didn't appreciate it. As he spoke, I realized the man had a series of fascinating artworks but was with the most unimpressive group of people ever.

Moving to Dubai

Leaving medical school to pursue a practice career was daunting. As an ambitious individual, I was torn between choosing a path that provided stability and a secure future. While the Republic of Iran had a lot to offer, I couldn't find the opportunities I craved there. The United States, on the other hand, seemed like the perfect place to cast my net and chase my dreams.

As an entrepreneur, I always have my eyes peeled for new possibilities to grow and expand my business. That's why I eventually decided to uproot my life and move to Dubai - a land of immense opportunity. The decision wasn't made lightly, but it felt natural.

Dubai is a city well-known for its thriving economy and business-friendly environment. Its strategic location at the crossroads of Europe, Asia, and Africa makes it a key gateway to these regions. It's become a bustling hub for trade and commerce as a result. The city's modern infrastructure and innovative focus were also huge draws for me, as they're crucial factors for any business looking to thrive in today's world.

But what sealed the deal for me was Dubai's entrepreneurial spirit. The city is home to a diverse community of ex-pats and locals who share a passion for business and innovation. Entrepreneurs have endless resources, including networking events, mentorship programs, and funding opportunities. A supportive environment makes launching and growing a business easier - exactly what I needed.

I can attest to the numerous benefits of my business located in this global hub for business, finance, and innovation.

And the best part? The city's favorable tax system means I can reinvest more money into my business and watch it grow even faster.

But it's not just about the practical benefits. Dubai's vibrant and diverse culture makes it a cosmopolitan and open-minded place to do business. Networking and building relationships are a breeze, thanks to people from all over the world living and working here.

Starting your business in Dubai could be your most valuable decision. It certainly was for me! So, if you're ready to take your business to the next level, consider your land of opportunity.

What Am I Saying in Essence?

Opportunities are phenomenal moments in life that have the potential to change everything. They can come in all shapes and sizes - from a chance encounter with a stranger to an unexpected problem that needs solving. These opportunities can arise from anywhere, be it from your strengths, a new technological breakthrough, or even a sudden market trend. By recognizing and seizing these opportunities, you can experience incredible growth, development, and success in every aspect of your life - from your career to your relationships. Identifying and taking advantage of these opportunities is a powerful skill that can be honed through a positive mindset and plenty of practice.

The mindset of opportunity is a game-changer that can revolutionize your life. It's an attitude that involves positivity, open-mindedness, and curiosity. With this mindset, you'll become a master at recognizing and seizing opportunities that come your way. Cultivating this approach is vital to develop the ability to spot and capitalize on opportunities, leading to an unparalleled level of success in life. So, if you're ready to unlock life's limitless possibilities, start cultivating the mindset of opportunity today!

If you want to be successful in life, you must learn to spot opportunities when they arise. These opportunities can be anything from a brilliant business idea to meeting someone who can change your life forever. However, it takes an open and curious mindset to recognize them. You need to pay attention to trends, be bold enough to ask questions, and take risks. With these qualities, you can discover opportunities that others might miss. The ability to recognize opportunities is a skill that you can sharpen with practice. It's a precious tool that can help you take your life to the next level and achieve your dreams.

The Stateless Millionaire is an Opportunist

The Stateless Millionaire is not your typical guy - they are a master of opportunity. To break boundaries and achieve financial freedom, you need a sharp eye for spotting opportunities that others miss. From Google to Amazon, the most influential brands in the world have one thing in common - they saw an opportunity where others saw none and seized it.

Take Steve Jobs and Steve Wozniak, for example - they revolutionized personal computing by cofounding Apple Computer. And who could forget Sara Blakely, the genius who saw a gap in the market for comfortable underwear for women?

But the Stateless Millionaire takes it to a new level. They see opportunities in circumstances and places where others see only obstacles. They are risk-takers who think outside the box and are not afraid to take calculated risks.

In today's interconnected world, the Stateless Millionaire understands that opportunities can be found in every corner of the globe. They see potential in emerging markets and developing economies. Others only see risk and uncertainty. They invest in the future, even when others hesitate.

The Stateless Millionaires have created some of the world's most successful businesses. They have disrupted industries, created new markets, and transformed the global economy. Their success is a testament to their ability to spot opportunities and turn them into reality.

Finally, on this

As I sit here, reflecting on my journey to success, one thing becomes crystal clear - opportunities are essential. Without them, we risk missing valuable chances to improve ourselves and our circumstances. But, with an open mind and the ability to spot growth and advancement opportunities, we can turn our wildest dreams into reality.

I remember the first time I took a chance on an opportunity that came my way. It was nerve-wracking, but I pushed myself to take the risk. And boy, am I glad I did! That one opportunity opened doors I never knew existed. It transformed my life and set me on a path to success.

In both my personal and professional lives, I actively seek out opportunities. I don't want to miss out on anything that could improve my circumstances or take me to new heights. It's not always easy, but I've learned that taking risks and trying new things is the only way to grow and achieve my goals.

So, to anyone reading this, I urge you to be ready to grab every opportunity that comes your way. Don't let fear or uncertainty hold you back. With each change comes growth and transformation. So, keep your mind clear and your eyes peeled, and be ready to watch your life unfold in incredible ways.

Conclusion

t is only after accomplishing a task that it dawns on you how rewarding achieving the task was. It would seem impossible at first. But once you reach the finish line, you could look back and say, "Wow, I can't believe I did it!" Becoming a stateless millionaire is a task you could accomplish irrespective of where you are. Ultimately, you'll look back and be glad you took the first step."

Becoming a stateless millionaire may seem impossible, but the rewards are immeasurable. Just like any goal worth pursuing, it takes diligent work, dedication, and risk-taking. Once you reach the finish line, you'll realize how rewarding the journey was.

As you navigate the ups and downs of building wealth and achieving financial freedom, it's easy to get bogged down in day-to-day struggles. But it's time to take a step back and look at the bigger picture. Every small step you take toward your goal brings you closer to it.

And once you achieve it, you'll look back in amazement at how far you've come. You'll remember the struggles, the setbacks, and the moments of doubt. You'll also see progress, wins, and moments of pure joy.

So if you're dreaming of becoming a stateless millionaire, don't let the initial impossibility discourage you. Take that first step and keep moving forward. It won't be easy, but the reward of achieving your goal is worth the effort. And when you reach the finish line, you'll look back and be glad you took that first step.

Looking back on my journey as a neurologist, entrepreneur, investor, author, and coach, I am thrilled. Writing this book allowed me to share my experiences and insights with you, hoping to inspire and guide them on their path to financial freedom.

I believe anyone can succeed if willing to learn.

Keep this in mind as you embark on your journey. Be open to new opportunities, stay committed to your vision, and don't fear calculated risks. Additionally, it's crucial to stay connected to the people and communities that matter to you. These connections provide the support and inspiration needed to achieve our wildest dreams.

I am grateful for the opportunity to share my stories and insights with you. And I am excited to see where your journey takes you. Remember, with the right mindset, a willingness to learn and grow, and a commitment to making a positive impact, you can become a stateless millionaire. You can also achieve your financial goals.

ABOUT THE AUTHOR

Ali Abkar is a well-known entrepreneur, investor, and author of "The Stateless Millionaire: Life's Lessons on How to Build Your Finances from Zero to Millions." He has over ten years of experience in establishing successful businesses, and his unique approach to entrepreneurship combines innovation, adaptability, and a comprehensive understanding of global markets.

Ali was born in Iran in the 1990s to an ordinary family. Due to his weak immune system, he spent most of his childhood at home. Despite facing numerous challenges, he obtained a doctorate in branding management and a second doctorate in business development management. He also studied medicine and neurology.

He learned to persevere and never give up, even in adversity. His life was filled with painful failures and joyous victories. He never gave up despite cancer, war, accidents, and political opposition. He believed he would not die until he changed the world.

Ali is a dreamer. He fought against disease in the hospital, hunger under an old bridge in Istanbul, dictatorship on the internet, and racism in foreign lands. He emerged victorious each time.

He lives by a simple principle that keeps him moving through every failure: "If I want, I have." He hopes to inspire others to do the same.

www.ingramcontent.com/pod-product-compliance
Lightning Source LLC
Chambersburg PA
CBHW071120160426
43196CB00013B/2649